Salt River Songs

to Hugh Rennie,
long-time friend

Sam Hunt

Salt River Songs

pb potton & burton

Contents

Sam Hunt, 2016. Photograph by Colin Hogg

Introduction

There is a lot of death in this collection of new poems by my friend Sam Hunt. It's easier to count the poems here that don't deal with the great destroyer than it is to point to the ones that do, but that's hardly surprising and Sam's not about to apologise for it.

He's 70 now and the end of things is on his mind. You might say he's getting a bit ahead of himself. Or you might say it's his new oeuvre – if you were moved to say such a thing, though perhaps best not if he's nearby. You don't hear a lot of French in Sam's part of the country, which is up north from almost everywhere else and over to the west a bit.

He lives, as he has always seemed to, floating at the edge of isolation, these days in the top half of a house at the end of a field, a few kilometres from the nearest small town, or, as he puts it, 'five gunshots from humanity'. And, naturally, less than a stone's throw from the salty water and the mangroves.

The downstairs of his house is empty. He has no interest in living there. He prefers to hang, upstairs with the view where he can gaze out to the horizon, find that halfway spot to turn his eye to, wait for a message, the brush of a wing on his shoulder, something to land. A pukeko possibly, or a poem. He waits around for those. They might be all he waits around for.

✳

The title poem of *Salt River Songs* is imbued with the place Sam's been living in now for longer than

7

anywhere he's lived since he was a boy at home with his mother and father in Milford, at the edge of the sea on Auckland's North Shore.

That's where it all started for him, with the poems, mostly told to him by his mother Betty. And then came Sam's discovery of his miracle memory and the connection he made to what he calls the old voices, never forgetting, for instance, hearing, for the first time, W.B. Yeats' 'The Collar-Bone of a Hare' and its world-shifting opening lines, which he'll say to this day at the very thought of them:

Would I could cast a sail on the water
Where many a king has gone
And many a king's daughter

And on he'll roll with the wonderful rest of it, unable to forget such lines because, as he says, they're unforgettable.

'You tell that poem to someone,' he says, 'and it has an effect. I'm constantly astonished.'

Being around Sam is also to be in a state of pretty much constant astonishment. Sam is himself with a totality that can overwhelm people. Part of the overwhelmingness is that many things about Sam have a mythic quality. His life spills into his poems and something spills back into his life from the poems themselves.

I've never been able to quite figure out how it works, but there's some magic at the middle of it. Sam is a master of making everything seem bigger, brighter, darker too.

And even just talking, when mere prose falls short of his needs, he reaches for poems. He seems to remember hundreds of them. Which is where the astonishment might come in. It still does for me, even after all this time and all those poems.

※

I've known him pretty well for around 30 years and not a lot has changed, just some of the detail. Sam lives alone. There's no letterbox at the top of his drive and no neighbours close enough to really be next door.

He still likes his shirts with the collars sticking up, a nod to his barrister father, who famously fathered Sam aged 60 and died 30 years later aged 90, when Sam was 30. The cosmic threes. It's the truth, but it's part of the myth too.

He lives the poet's life. He truly does.

'I never really considered anything else,' he says. But how could he?

He's timeless and he's a man out of time, though not running out of time, not yet. Most of his reference points are the old voices, Yeats, James K. Baxter, Denis Glover, Alistair Te Ariki Campbell. Many others, mostly dead.

He recently went to the first feature film he's seen in a cinema in decades. It was over in Dargaville and it blew him away, though he'd previously not liked going to the movies much, being uneasy about sitting with all those strangers in the dark.

'But I must do that again,' he said afterwards. 'Maybe we could go when you come up.'

※

'It's not an interview is it?' Sam wanted to know when I mentioned I'd like to come and visit him.

'No,' I said. 'It's far too late for that sort of thing. I'm just coming to check that you're actually there.'

It's quite a long way to go just for that, 10 hours on the road from where I live to where he lives, half a country away.

I'd told Sam I might take a photo of him and he seemed fine about that. But when I arrive at his place and there he is, outside his back door grinning a greeting, something is not quite right about his face. I notice this straight away, as any person intending to take photos of someone's face should, though I don't say anything at first. I just bring my stuff upstairs, join him in a drink, gaze out at the view.

'I love living here,' he says, following my stare.

Another drink. I tell him I'm going to cook him a curry for dinner. I've brought the makings.

'You should start on that before you drink too much more,' says Sam. 'You might forget to cook.'

As I drift to the kitchen, he adds, 'Feel free to take your photos whenever you like.'

'I'm afraid I can't,' I tell him.

'Why not?'

'I think you know why. I can't photograph you in that state.'

'What state?'

'You appear to be growing what I can only describe as a moustache.'

He fixes me with that icy look of his.

'You cheeky little shit. What do you want me to do?'

'I'd like you to get rid of it.'

'You actually want me to have a shave?'

'I actually do, if it's not too much trouble.'

Sam stamps off towards the bathroom, growling and muttering.

'It's for your own good,' I tell his back, though I might be going a bit far now. It's just that he flirted with a moustache a few years ago and, unfortunately it ended up co-starring in *Purple Balloon and Other Stories*, a documentary feature film made about him at the time. I remind him of this.

'You don't want to go down in posterity as a man with a moustache,' I shout towards the bathroom, but he's too taken up with shaving to say any more.

He emerges after five minutes all pink and smooth.

'You're a bit shiny now.'

'Don't push it.'

※

Through a low window upstairs, I can see a family of hares disporting themselves on Sam's lawn, their huge ears upright, glowing red in the light from the low sun. The hares seem a little spooky, considering Yeats and that poem.

'They come out every evening about this time,' says Sam.

Would I could cast a sail on the water
Where many a king has gone
And many a king's daughter,
And alight at the comely trees and the lawn
The playing upon pipes and the dancing,
And learn the best thing is
To change my loves while dancing
And pay but a kiss for a kiss.

I would find by the edge of that water
The collar-bone of a hare
Worn thin by the lapping of water,
And pierce it through with a gimlet and stare
At the old bitter world where they marry in churches,
And laugh over the untroubled water
At all who marry in churches,
Through the white thin bone of a hare.

And make of that what you will, but it does have an effect, especially when Sam sails into it. I do eventually get back to cooking the curry, but dinner is late, the sun has sunk and the hares are long curled up in their hare beds.

※

In 1988, for the purpose of writing a biography of Sam, I signed on as his road manager for one of his tours. I won't claim I was a natural road manager, but I got the job done and managed to write a book at the same time.

The big thing was that we got along well. I learned a great deal. We felt like we were a gang at times and maybe we were. And then there was another tour when the book, *Angel Gear*, came out and then maybe another. Or did we go back out on the road just for the sake of it?

I'm not sure, but my life has never quite been the same since. It goes almost without saying that Sam Hunt is a very dangerous person to know, though, oddly, his mother Betty, normally a wise owl, was inclined to blame me for leading her boy astray.

She came along to the launch of *Angel Gear*, and chided me for the bad language in the book.

'A few too many fucks,' she said. She liked the book, though. She thought it got to something, but really Sam got there first and I was just taking notes.

There is a bit in the book about a reporter interviewing Sam and asking him, 'Do you write typically New Zealand poetry?'

Sam: 'I can't answer that. I don't know what typically New Zealand poetry is … Denis Glover once said to me, "Sambo, the toughest poems to write are the simple ones".'

Then, when the reporter had emptied her bag of dull questions and gone away to find out who Denis Glover was, Sam told me:

'I remember meeting Denis Glover for the first time. One of my cousins by marriage is married to Allen Curnow, the poet, and when I was about 17, I visited them on one of my lone voyages.

'I walked from Bethels down to Karekare – took about four or five days over it, spending a night at Anawhata. I stayed with Jennifer and Allen Curnow at Karekare, and late at night this car arrived.

'Curnow said to me, "Here Sam, you take the torch and see who's out there."

'The last of the braves.

'And here was a very pissed man getting out of a taxi. Owed a massive amount of money. He'd driven out from Auckland. It was Denis Glover. He'd come up from Wellington on the train.

'Pissed with poems spilling out. He'd just written one, which was later published, about a boy bouncing a ball against a cenotaph. They sat up and drank.

'Next morning Glover was up really early. We went down to the beach and I dived for mussels …

'Glover really had his finger on it. He'd say things like, "Don't ever become too respectable." Sure, he accepted a few honours, but he was still right outside the law.

'And, at his best, a fucking wonderful poet. The classics, everybody knows them, like "The Magpies". But they are classics. Lines like, "… Yet thinking of my dear damned dead/Friends who sailed on a Friday."

'Fucking good. In just a few phrases he knocks completely out the window all the theories about New Zealand poetry.'

※

Sam has strong feelings regarding theories about New Zealand poetry. He has strong feelings about academia and those who specialise in pulling apart poems, analysing, theorising, summarising, surmising. They spoil everything by missing the whole point – which is simply the poem.

And Sam did take Denis Glover's suggestion from all those years ago and never became too respectable. Well, actually, not really even remotely respectable, though his landlord recently installed a heat pump for him, something Robbie Burns could only have dreamed of.

I'm not inclined to think a little comfort will turn away the arrival of new poems. Some of those here in *Salt River Songs* arrived fully formed, others in stops and starts.

These new poems together add up to a powerful dose from my plugged-in pal. There might be a lot

to do with death in this collection, but there is also
something even bigger – a sense of timeless wonder.
Like in 'Six Sestets', where Sam says:

> *You can see how it works,*
> *how the spin of the Earth*
>
> *is all to do with the spiders*
> *spinning webs*
> *so delicate*
> *they trap the light:*

There is so much love of life in those words, it
helps me bear all the talk of death in here. And, of
course, it's just talk.

Later in the evening, revived by my curry,
Sam says, 'I think I'm doing reasonably well –
considering the passing of time.'

Though it's only half past seven.

– Colin Hogg, 2016

Salt river songs

1.
Never the sparkling waters
or the beautiful daughters

as sparkling as they be –
it's a muddy creek for me

twisting and turning
on Kaipara time

floating down stream.
On the next tide, returning.

2.
The Landing built roughly
where early settlers landed –

months at sea behind them,
more months' uncertainty.

They ended up in a land
they never had in mind.

I'll be leaving by the Landing
on Kaipara time.

3.
A fisherman from Pahi
got a mermaid in his net –

good as a man can get
when he falls in love at sea

on Kaipara time,
the nets well set: that,

and immaculate
timing of tides.

4.
On Kaipara time
a patriach lay dying –

tears for what he'd done,
the cheating and lying –

family gathered round him
he said, I know I'm dying.

There's only one problem:
I can't. But, God, I'm trying.

5.
On Kaipara time
he died and the family

joined hands like the five
salt rivers of the Kaipara

each of them knowing
it would soon be for them

the tidal clocks chime
on Kaipara time.

6.
I see you up in town,
we meet on the street:

good to see you I say,
you say it's good to see me.

You're moving east you tell me.
I wish you a clear sea …

meantime, Kaipara time,
it's a muddy creek for me.

Tomorrow, or today (1)

What a fine day a man is singing
with all his heart on radio
what a fine day it is
I could climb the Tower of Pisa
set fire to the Mona Lisa
and at the end of the day
we'll be able to say
What a fine day it was,
what a fine day, but for Mona.

Don't get me wrong, I never
planned it this way. Who would have –
with mere flick of wrist –
thought it could all turn to shit, oh
so like the showman said!
What else the showman said
I never quite heard and was
sorry to miss – some will say
it's better not to know …

So come here and lay your
invisible self down –
there's no one around, there
hasn't been for years.
But for the man singing
with all his heart on radio –
I keep getting the feeling
he knows what he needs to:
that it's such a fine day

he made up a song
and sang it with a heart
no one's likely to forget.
On fine days they gather
in Paris and Pisa and
down at the wharf at Pahi:
at the end of each day, say
I hope he
keeps singing that song.

Tomorrow, or today (2)

We prepare for departure,
no see-you-later;
we make our goodbyes.
It's a quiet time, quieter
    by hour, by day,
    by day, by hour:
not a lot left to say.

I was moving the cattle earlier,
told them We're in this together,
we're headed for the Works,
no one pumping the brakes:
    no one, I told them,
    is giving a damn –
the stock truck's on its way.

And later found myself talking
to nodding tops of totara:
told them I'd no idea
how all of this started, or how
    (when it does) it stops.
    The trees agreed.
And it just got quieter.

Tomorrow, or today (3)

The wounded will say
we know you don't want us

but we're with you, brother,
all of the way

is how it is.

The wounded were right –
they weren't what we wanted,

tonight, or any other.
We wanted them dead,

was how it was.

Tomorrow, or today (4)

You know, I wrote
the first email ever,

wrote it on the trot
somewhere between now & never.

Recipient?
None other

than my late mother.
And her reply: 'Repent, son, repent!'

Tomorrow, or today (5)

The young ones wondering
how long they've got to live,
cook with canola
or should it be olive?

Up at the old folks' home
out on the big verandah,
we don't need to wonder.
We know.

Tomorrow, or today (6)

I find I've a growing
liking for flags,
flagpoles & all.

They tell me
this gusterly late day –
half-mast or full –

a local has died,
or hasn't.
And which way

the wind's blowing.

I live in hope

I live in hope –
poet, preacher,
Bishop, Cardinal, Pope –

who knows,
could one day get the Big Nod –
God.

I live in hope,
and in love, elope
with an angel.

Death called by

i.m. Glenn Jowitt

Death called by the other day –
no one was home at the time.
A note, 'Sorry I missed you',
stuck under the front door mat.

I'm sorry I missed him too.
I would have asked him on in,
told him to kick off his boots
& leave his scythe at the gate.

We would have had a catch-up;
maybe rolled up a number.
I'd tell him I was pissed off
at the friends he'd taken out.

Death would have – passing the joint –
agreed: it was just a job
he was sent here to do.
Then would ask, 'What about you?'

Acquinas, at the fireplace

He looked in the fireplace,
embers purple and red and all
he saw was his face.
And though little –

like six, maybe seven –
he knew from what he could tell,
no way was this Heaven.
It had to be Hell.

At the top of the stair

Two empty boots,
two empty bottles

and a man on his own
who thought the stairway

would take him to Heaven.
Which is why he

kicked off his boots, why he
drank the wine he did.

Some said
that's why he died –

he should have kept his boots on.

The folk, though, on this occasion,
got it wrong. His feet were sore,

he was tired as he
had ever been. And the wine,

and the where,
and the when?

They're there,
at the top of the stair.

My father's waistcoats

My father's waistcoats
never had pockets.

It was years later
someone explained

a good lawyer in court
didn't need notes ...

I never went with the law
like my father would have liked.

But I got to swing juries –
like he said – swinging the lead.

I never rode into town
like I'd like to have done.

But I carry a gun
in my head.

Voznesensky

Voznesensky
    meeting his girlfriend in the rain

is taking place tonight.
    There's the same

telephone box, late fifties,
    Voznesensky & girlfriend

rooting like rattlesnakes.
    The whole world is shaking.

Voznesensky himself is
    shaking.

It must be love, he thought.
    Or a bad night.

Or good news
    breaking.

Just in case

Why people bother
    to look for the lost ones,
we never were sure:

    as sure as someone wins
someone else loses,
    as soon as the moon is

full, red as it is,
    it wanes.
Everything says

    the lost are lost,
there is no finding them,
    there is no way home:

a fishermen dead, wet sand,
    a five-year-old
taken by a rogue wave.

    But we keep on looking.
Tonight, under a blood moon.
    Just in case.

Exit lines for an ex

1.
The clouds won't lift
not as forecasted:
shadows show no shift
theories get blasted

nothing is fact –
I tell you that.
And if we must split,
so be it.

2.
You have something to say?
you won't have it said
you hung around
till the last man was dead;
that you hit the ground

running, running so fast
you went the wrong way –
ended up in my past –
what you hoped was tomorrow
was only yesterday

repeated and repeated,
the number of men dead,
the hard luck stories
of the cheated and defeated.
You have something to say?

From the end of the wharf

He was, I guess, the unofficial
leader of the gang – the kids
who broke the by-laws daily
jumping off the end of the wharf.

Random weekends a Council
Inspector would arrive, record
names and addresses of offenders
rounded up at the foot of the wharf.

My friend was always up there,
first one to give them the facts –
would say he was an orphan,
that he lived by himself.

It never seemed to matter
how often the Council hit,
he'd tell the same story,
mostly get away with it.

A few friends from childhood
tell me he stayed the same –
the right word, always,
always as it was.

He comes to mind, the boy,
jumping, for all his worth –
ashes, today, dropped off
from the end of the wharf.

Immaculate

It phased her out,
the word 'immaculate':
she thought I thought
she was of such state.

Which was not
close to what I meant:
but close as I got
to that high sacrament.

Bride among brides

Once a year I'd see her
in my son's class photograph –

the dark one always
at the edge of the picture;

knew she'd break hearts.
(Time has its way.)

Today, in the 'Newly Weds',
bride among brides ...

From her local marae
you hear the Tasman

smashing itself to pieces;
reminded,

if you don't breathe
deep as the sea,

you die.

Six sestets

1.
A skyful of cloud breaks up,
scatters out to sea,

gives the sun fair go.
My shadow

resumes itself.
I can do with the company.

2.
So, no,
you're right, I never
pine to see the sea:

enough to know
it's around the next corner,
left past the cabbage tree.

3.
You get up early, you see

the world is held together
by cobwebs
and on mornings clear as this –
this, the start of winter –
you can see how it works.

4.
You can see how it works,
how the spin of the Earth

is all to do with the spiders
spinning webs
so delicate
they trap the light:

5.
they trap the light
and hold it
tight ...
so, no,
you're right,

I don't

6.
pine for the sea:
the gravel road I'm on,
the next corner
left past the cabbage tree –

and keeping up, my shadow –
is all I need know.

Tell me what

Tell me what I don't know –
not what I know now

or what I'll know tomorrow.
Tell me something new,

a story that will blow
this steady head apart.

Which is where
the best stories start:

you go on, and on,
talking of the morning after:

the storm, the break-up at sea.
And all of it gone,

gone down deep
where no one should go –

gone as that! ... Tell me
what I won't know tomorrow.

Like, what it was like

We live close to death, old mate,
without even knowing it –

I discovered the other
morning a white-tail spider,

sitting just centimetres
from where I reach for the glass.

So close to death, my friend,
but now, instead, the real thing –

as living was, as dying is –
with a love that gave us song,

reason to rhyme, or just sing
some song someone somewhere sang.

We stand around at graveyards,
workers waiting for the bus.

It's okay, we're going the
same way. Some even hitchhike,

go out with a friend, for the
last time. Like, what it was like.

Home thoughts, 2015

International
passenger jets fly over at
35,000 feet –
faster than the speed of sound.

I like to watch them
and listen at the same time –
simultaneously and
both feet on the ground –

listening, then just after,
for the supersonic boom.
And not a thought
of leaving home.

Piping the fife

I won't wave ferns, pipe the fife,
there'll be no intake of breath:
I never liked you in life,
I do not like you in death.

Yes, I know the town stopped still
when word came through you were dead.
If you'd asked them how they feel
they would've told you – elated.

The Anglican Cathedral
is expected to be full:
everybody in town
wants to bear witness you're gone.

Which is all as it should be.
We each get on with our life
as well as we can. For me,
I lie low, piping the fife.

Assisi

The man who sang
to his brother, Sun,

poured out his heart
to big sister, Moon.

He also had a song –
my mother, a convert,

often used to quote,
I think in Italian –

ask for nothing,
and refuse nothing.

Lines for Lyn

i.m. Lyndon Wilson

Lyn – it looks like the tide
is just about out.
It comes back in again
for those that come later,

without a doubt: without a doubt
we've no need to bother.
And as for 'the other side' –
I'll spot you there, brother.

In a dream my father

In a dream my father says
(speaking to my mother)

You can't recall the whole of
Lycidas by heart, can you?

And (in the dream) my mother
recites the whole of it,

Yet once more, O ye Laurels,
and once more, ye Myrtles brown ...

my mother tells it, line 1
to line 193,

to fresh Woods and Pastures new.
And (in the dream) my father

promises my mother the Woods.
If she can live with his Moods.

We had a horse

1.
We had a horse, Phar Lap,
his stride, perfect as it gets.
As for me, it's the last lap –
a good gallop,
few worries, no regrets.

2.
We had a horse. He gave –
when times were merciless –
people reason to live.
He gave us punters hope;
more or less.

3.
We had a horse. And that,
for us,
mattered more than a house.
You can't ride a house
out of town.

To have been

To have *been there and done*
whatever *that* was

was an achievement
rarely seen in these parts.

It was a ceremony
where people took themselves

so
seriously

I got to wonder what
got me in this spot.

Then made a run for it.

Then again

We were
talking of life
how some believe
there's more,

that
death isn't it.
Some of the time
I envy them:

but this morning it
doesn't seem to matter.
I tell myself
live for the moment!

then again,
why worry when
all there is to do
is die?

Nurse Hayes musings

1.
Nurse Hayes asked me
who was I ringing?

I told her
my father.

She said that can't be.
Your father he

would be all thirty years dead
was what Nurse Hayes said.

2.
I told her
you give me the shits

and went ahead and
dialled his number –

all of five digits –
but his number was engaged.

Which came as no surprise,
at least to Nurse Hayes.

3.
Later in the dayroom
a message came through –

a phone call for me,
my father somebody thought.

And it was,
it was my father;

we were
talking to each other.

4.
He asked was I writing poems?
He seemed to think I was.

I can't remember now
the rest that was said:

but before Hayes
cut my father off,

I did get to ask him,
What's it like dead?

The Big Beyond

What's that country through the Pass –
the Big Beyond – what's it like?

no one we know made it back,
no one, not once, to tell us.

Here, heresy & hearsay,
passed on by the dead strangers.

For me, I've my own ideas:
one, to ride the Pass someday.

If any of them

If any of them were to know
the pain still to come –

that waits patiently outside – they'd
end it then, end it there.

The heads of nodding totara

tell me this, this wild westerly morning.
They tell me no one should have stayed.

After drought

1.
Out on the paddock
a shot of light
catches your eye:

you think, what is it?
it's a puddle the rain
left when it left,
first rain

since God took the kid.

2.
Why we never died
doing what we did

OK at the time,
not now. Was that

a smile or grimace

I saw under gibbous moonlight?
Was it even your face?

Too late now,
too late to know.

3.
You praise
'God's world'

you sing a song,
'God's world'.

Someone somewhere says
you've got it wrong;

word is
the world is

God.

4.
God doesn't live here.
Not anymore.

One day, 'out of the blue'
we got the nod,

to say Thanks, folks,
thanks for believing

& I wouldn't be leaving.
But the old man says I've got to.

Then, like any con,
God was gone,

the kid with him.

A shot of light
that caught the eye.

This time of year

It's the time of year
bush fires rage
the time of year the smoke
is blown from Australia
the whole way over the Tasman;
the time of year
with the sun going orange at sunset

and my father saying
'it's those Australian fires again
blowing in from the Tasman';
when I knew, without being told,
my father wasn't just old,
the old man was wise; knew
which way the wind blew;

where the smoke came from and why
the setting sun turned orange.
And the name of the mountain range –
the one lying east to nor'west,
the range no one else noticed –
he knew them by their first names.
As they knew his.

You start taking notice.
And you know Australia's
west across the Tasman.
Where the smoke comes from –
too close to home.
Like all of us, brothers and sisters,
like all of us

this time of year.

It was a good night

Riding with the sun behind
casting a shadow that gets smaller
the faster I go:

I was doing over 200 kilometres an hour,
220 say.
I'd caught up with my shadow.

But not until
the guests came in and started talking
of me, the man in the box,

what a good bloke I'd been –
sadly missed I heard
somebody say –

that I knew this was death
and I was part of it.
On this occasion, all of it.

It was a good night
to get hammered.

Song for a post-modernist

1.
How does
the next poem go?

you're back, man,
where you began.

Before anything is born,
it dies.

2.
So how
the next poem has

nothing to do with you,
it has to do

with all of us.
Not later. Now.

3.
I wonder
what you're doing;

trying to remember
what day it is?

It's your birthday,
yes!

4.
Old folk keep forgetting
pin-numbers and passwords.

Of course they do.
They've seen disaster

coming from a long way off.
They're not crying; they're laughing.

Past the last stop

I had a friend who lived
a half-hour walk
past the last bus stop.

We walked it together
so often I cannot
forget every step.

We talked of poems,
the shape of the shore,
the tide that gave it shape.

I wonder what happened,
what of him?
past the last stop, Long Bay,

Byzantium.

A *minute after*

A minute after hearing car
turn from gravel road to drive –
low gear down to the house –
I catch a glimpse of light:

reflection of sun on chrome.
It stops where I am –
the boy home safe.
I find myself blessing myself:

knowing well could be
this never was happening.
Something different, entirely,
telephone ringing,

somewhere, someone:
bring back, bring back,
please, bring back that
young son to me.

What can a young man do?

When it was more or less
time to leave school
the folk would always ask
what I wanted to do?

Climb a tree that no one
had ever climbed –
to the top of it –
and see out there an ocean

none of them believed in.
And what then?
the same folk would be asking.
And I would ask them back: what

can a young man do but
jump for it?

On the move

The wound – more like an eye –
stared back at me.
It would not close.

It stayed open
looking straight back as if
to say:

if you don't like
the look of me can I suggest
you fuck off.

Which was the best
advice I'd had in years.
I headed West.

The wound, I heard word,
closed over.
But I keep on the move.

I was waiting

i.m. Graham Brazier

I was waiting for the phone to ring.
You were busy dying.
Connections never happened,
door left unopened.

You were waiting for the angels to sing
but could only hear crying.
Do we see each other again?
I guess, by now, you know

answers to the questions
we spent lives looking for.
Do we see each other again?
I guess you'll know by now.

The wind's a sou'wester –
it's pummelling the totara,
prize-fighter it is.
Totara don't stand a chance!

And you're busy dying.
And I don't know if it's
the wind in my eyes, or rain,
but I can't stop crying.

The good luck song

We get to know each other
slowly
     as tide rising over rocks.
That's on a still day. On
a stormy one it's something
different. It's
        fuckfuckfuck.

I walk on the shoreline as
often as I can and tides
allow:
     often enough,
when it's low, see
a shadow in the shallows
quick as a flounder
        and just about as pretty:

knowing it's waiting the tide
that matters; that after that, it's just
     luckluckluck.

Tell me something new

Tell me something new, doctor,
no more bad news.
I'm as tired of that as I'm
sure you are.

Let's try to make it in alive
was what I thought this morning
as I was tossed by waves ashore.
It was a waking like no other –

and, doctor, did I know it!
I staggered into the day, the bay –
it mattered neither way –
light or dark, I didn't care.

Then somebody stopped me.
It was my mother, Betty.
We hugged. 'About time,' she said.
The rest is history.

No poem

I went outside
thinking there could be a poem
buried in the long grass
or down the bank to the river.

I scrambled down
swinging totara trunk to totara trunk
and landed on my arse
in thick Kaipara mud.

There was no poem to be had.

Crap, cry, crucify

were the first words I heard
first thing this morning
banging through the head
between darkness & light.

The 'crap' – to do with a poem
I'd tried to make up last night.
In the first light re-read it.
It was crap alright.

The 'cry' is the cry
of those still living – you hear it? –
the cry that makes men sing;
to hit it hard; to tune into

the nervous
system of the universe.
And 'crucify'?
We never liked the bastard.

Both boots

Talking of my new book
a friend remarks
there's death on every page.

I'm sorry, Pedro,
I never meant it to be,
but it is how it is:

death lurking and leering
each turn of page.
Even some seepage.

You go on: impossible
questions that have no answers.
Death is there – sure.

As is life – what little
I can recall right now.
The poems say so too.

Or did, last time I heard them
giggling and rehearsing
just out the back of this place –

all stoned, a bit too early, eh Pedro!
As for me, I like to keep
an eye on the clock;

keep, well as I can,
both boots on the ground.

And if so

I wonder where
friends that were
have disappeared to:

some I guess are
dead – but nobody noticed.
Others, you

particularly, what happened there?
Did you disappear
under low-pressure air,

marry money, who knows,
go overseas or
back to the street?

wonder, too,
do you still write poems? Or
read them, even?

I hope you do.
And if so,
you stumble on this one.

For the one

I like the half light –
or is that half dark?

I find it's
easy on the eyes:
not too light, not
too dark, no

day no night.
I like it this way,
can see
all I need to.

And what about you?
a night owl you say!

with those wide eyes
I guess you could be.
Who'd want to be a mouse
with you hovering!

I'll stay the man I am,
it's got to be safer.
And I like it safe,
enough of the rough.

What say we go out tonight?
I walk, okay? You can fly.

Too many to name

There's no counting the dead
and those still living
have other things to do:

feed the child – the only
other survivor on the block –
from a family she knows

nothing of:
too many to name.
She holds the child close.

Which can only be
what this is about –
holding the child close.

Cameras move in
but can't get near her.
She's seen all the grief

there is to see.
She knows there's no
counting the dead.

Too many to name.
Too many.
Aamene.

Running out of time

You could say I'm
    running out of time.
You do say
    precisely that, you say I'm
    running out of time.

I like it this way.
    It's how it always should have been.
But never was, was it?
    There was rot in the beams,
    nights full of bad dreams.

I saw you the other day.
    I think it was you.
You had your bossy look on.
    I kept well out of sight
    as you strode by ...

liking this life in the tree tops
    buffeted by any wind blowing,
and like the drive to the shops
    knowing there's no way of knowing
    if this could be it:

greeting a few friends –
    this is how it ends, this is how it ends.
Everyone knows but no one is showing.
    Everyone knows it's not a joint glowing
    but time running out.

Other work by Sam Hunt

From Bottle Creek: Selected Poems 1967–69 (1969)

Bracken Country (1971)

From Bottle Creek (1972)

Roadsong Paekakariki (1973)

South Into Winter: Poems and Roadsongs (1973)

Time to Ride (1975)

Drunkard's Garden (1977)

Collected Poems 1963–1980 (1980)

Running Scared (1982)

Approaches to Paremata (1985)

Selected Poems (1987)

Making Tracks (1991)

Down the Backbone (1995)

Roaring Forties (1997)

James K. Baxter: Poems selected and introduced by Sam Hunt (2008)

Doubtless: New and selected poems (2008)

Backroads: Charting a Poet's Life (2009)

Chords & Other Poems (2011)

Knucklebones: Poems 1962–2012 (2012)

Published in 2016 by Potton & Burton
98 Vickerman Street, PO Box 5128, Nelson, New Zealand
www.pottonandburton.co.nz

Some of these poems have appeared in the *Listener*, the *Paparoa Press*, the Phantom Billstickers *Café Reader*, on Radio New Zealand and on the *Spinoff* website. 'I live in hope' and 'Both boots' have appeared as Phantom Billstickers.

© Introduction, Colin Hogg
© Sam Hunt

ISBN 978 0 947503 03 1

Printed in New Zealand by printing.com